The Thousand Wells

The Thousand Wells

POEMS

Adam Kirsch

WINNER OF THE NEW CRITERION POETRY PRIZE

Ivan R. Dee

CHICAGO 2002

To Remy

THE THOUSAND WELLS. Copyright © 2002 by Adam Kirsch. All rights reserved, including the right to reproduce this book or portions thereof in any form. For information, address: Ivan R. Dee, Publisher, 1332 North Halsted Street, Chicago 60622. Manufactured in the United States of America and printed on acid-free paper.

Library of Congress Cataloging-in-Publication Data:
Kirsch, Adam, 1976–
    The thousand wells : poems / Adam Kirsch.
        p. cm.
    "Winner of the New Criterion Poetry Prize."
    ISBN 1-56663-451-2 (alk. paper)
        I. Title.

PS3611.I77 T48 2002
811'.6—dc21   2002023430

Contents

I

Arcadia (Spring)	9
Arcadia (Autumn)	11
Welcome	13
Pollution	14
The Patient Lookers	15
Away	16
The Beginning	17
Balsam	20

II

Bacchus	23
The Dawn	25
Heroes Have the Whole Earth for Their Tomb	28
Three Odes after Horace	30
Washington	34
Goodbye to Washington	37

Y2K   39
Lebanon   41
The Chosen People   42

III

Autobiography   47
One Weekend   49
Waking   53
Post-Mortem   54
A Love Letter   55
Epithalamium   60

IV

Emblems   65
Indecision   66
Irresponsible Foetus   68
Zoloft   69
Spring Forward   71
42 Up   73
Don Giovanni   75
Going to Bed   76

Acknowledgments

Grateful acknowledgment is made to the publications where some of these poems first appeared: *Harvard Review* ("Autobiography"), *The Formalist* ("*Don Giovanni*"), *The Paris Review* ("Arcadia (Spring)" and "Balsam"), *Partisan Review* ("Heroes Have the Whole Earth for Their Tomb"), and *Seneca Review* ("The Chosen People").

I

Arcadia (Spring)

Now that on Cedar Hill the trees
Regain in April shower and breeze
Their winter-severed canopies,

And on the rooftops bedded flowers
Exfoliate in sunlit hours
Or drowse in the shade of water-towers,

Somehow notorious Central Park
Where men would hesitate to walk
In the murderous, abandoned dark

Becomes a remembered garden, where
Even defenseless women dare
To lie undressed in the open air;

Under the cradling firmament
Bodies remember or invent
The postures of supreme content,

Sexual languor, infant sprawl:
Where pain was individual
Animal good unites us all.

But whether this is the earliest
Precarious instinctive trust
By mind corrupted and repressed,

Or that millennia too late
We learn a while to sublimate
The ancient drive to violate,

How can the day end otherwise
Than every previous paradise?
Love from its own perfection dies,

As spring against the stronger
Predatory summer
Fights briefly and goes under.

Arcadia (Autumn)

Seen from above with cartographic eye
The park would lie silent, parcelled and controlled;
Seen from a bench among the passersby
It is various to me and random as the world.

This Sunday morning, unobservant pairs
Of lovers, in each other's eyes complete,
Stroll arm in arm the asphalt thoroughfares,
Or stop a while by a secluded seat;

Mothers in thrall to their imperial
Children are patient with unjust demands,
While the lesser orders, plant and animal,
Condemned to a language no one understands,

Seem the luckier, the self-contented creatures.
Each visible thing in its accustomed motion,
In its appropriate and changeless features,
Obeys for a while its nature and its notion,

As though this fraction of the world could run
Perpetually in accustomed courses,
Like planets in their race around the sun,
Only indentured to eternal forces.

Nothing this morning more incredible
Than the one fact in which we must believe,
That everything human and celestial
Moves only in a limited reprieve

From the common sentence; as the stars above
Totter in turn and fall, so here below
This pageantry of nature and of love
Lives in its dying. May its death be slow.

Welcome

Welcome them all again: the weatherman
　　At break of day, his smiling mild prediction;
The usual strangers elbowing for place
　　As the train screams and hisses in the station;

The urine-sweet that breaks the sweat-stale air
　　And out to the city's panelled brilliancy,
The day's few moments out-of-doors, below
　　A cold and tower-broken canopy.

All these, the garments once of something vast,
　　Remote, almost surrendering to sight—
These million stains and shades that once concealed
　　An undivided and eternal light—

Can these bleach, fade and fray? Grow dim, grow dull?
　　Or are there secrets still, if we dare to question—
As salmon, in the stagnant pool unseen,
　　Glitter and glide in the gull's patient vision?

Pollution

If there were nothing here to shed its light
Carelessly skyward, as the evening came,
Something would be revealed of such a height
To put our towers to shame;

Something I've rarely seen, but can recall
As a distant script, a destined way, a band
That holds us to a brightness over all,
A huge unerring hand.

Such clean and unaccommodating skies
Are gone, but not lamented. We would rather
Cover ourselves with human things, that rise
So far and no farther.

The Patient Lookers

Praise to the patient lookers: they
Who find the repetitious play
Of sunlight on a bale of hay

Enough of being to amaze,
To fix the self-forgetting gaze
That makes of pure attention praise:

They are rewarded here below.
Others, unsuited for the slow
Unfolding of that kingly show,

Bypass seductions of detail;
Their vision, rapid, prying, pale,
Urges the tearing of the veil,

Sure that behind a gorgeous screen
The substances of things unseen
Are trying to tell us what they mean,

In characters the whole world tall.
These pity; for the message shall
Come clear elsewhere, or not at all.

Away

Tonight, when the city's titan towers
Shine out as pure matter, glass and steel,
Proclaiming indisputable powers,
Standard and guardian of the real;

When higher visions are withdrawn
In anger to their fastnesses,
And earth, forgetting they have gone,
Is lost among grosser presences;

When science is called to ascertain
The true, and all the rest is story,
And the bodies of the dead remain
But not their grave defiant glory;

Now, come! After wandering here so long,
I ignore every evidence, and pray:
From this place where the heart does not belong,
Come, spirit me silently away.

The Beginning

Fall, winter, spring—each season has been passed
In the city now, and summer comes again.
First summer night! And in the street, the last
Of the couples strolling still at half past ten;
Reaching her door, they move to part, and then
Give in just once more to the evening's pull,
For it is still warm, and their hearts are full.

This is the day of solstice. Now the sun
Stands motionless at the pivot of the year,
Or seems to stand; we know it has begun
Even tonight to feel itself too near,
And, having spent six months in traveling here,
Is willing to grant the fullness of its grace
One day, and then begins to hide its face.

Fall, winter, spring. Each season has arrived
With a promise to create the world anew,
Each in his image; for a year I've lived
Hoping that their transforming power would do
For me what my own strength can't carry through,
The total reversal and deliberate change
Of the daily world to something rich and strange,

As though in another weather, different light,
Possibilities that had been long concealed
From my inward-turning and habitual sight
Would be in blazing panoply revealed;
But now I've seen all that the year can yield;
Tonight four seasons with their hopes are gone,
And the mind ends as it started, still my own.

In the sky, late violet is turning black.
The world continues its appointed round,
Now facing sunward, now turning its back,
Circling in circles, to its circle bound;
Nor after laboring aeons has it found
A pattern more various than night and day,
Summer and winter, towards and then away.

Below, I think about the course I've run
From the last solstice to this shrunken night.
Is there a day in which I haven't done
Some shameful thing in my own or others' sight
In pursuit of a vague, illusory delight?
So many times, imagining release
In triumphant ambition or exhausted peace,

I tried to forget myself: now in the dark
With force, imploring, promises, attack;
Now hoping that sincerity and work
Would make up for the easy grace I lack;
And now at the desk, surrounded by a stack
Of impressive books, believing I could read
Enough to supply the spirit's speechless need.

All year I've followed a more manifold
And wilder circuit. But the narrow mind
I have been given is no less controlled
By established orbits; nor can I, designed
For a lifetime of becoming, hope to find
The inconceivable, storied prodigy
Of flesh or spirit that will let me be.

Think of the sun, arriving to bestow
No greater light than the world is capable
Of bearing, and at once making to go;
So every light to us; impossible
To seize on the earth some more desirable,
Intenser illumination; our sublime
Exists, if at all, only like us, in time.

More time is coming. Soon the summer days
Again give way to autumn's sharper air,
Autumn that brings to harvest and decays
Into purer winter, stripping branches bare
Till the irresistible spring shows blossoms there;
There is no moment of eternal good
In the cycle of vacancy and plenitude.

Only tonight, upon the final hour
Of solstice, let me think of it again —
One backward look at the imagined power
Whose supplicant I have too often been;
With a new season, let new work begin,
And in place of the mind's impossibilities
Let stand the unending fullness of what is.

Balsam

But look, there—who is that one, hurrying
Around the corner, swallowed by the crowd?
Already his face is vague—the only thing
I can remember is his voice, not loud,
His coat pulled tight around him, his head bowed,
As though he would have made himself so small
The world could not be sure that he was there at all.

Oh, but I know him! In this gentle street,
That sometimes seems too full of gentleness,
He tramples the gifts lying at his feet;
Wounded somehow, he feeds on his distress
And is not nourished. In his loneliness
He raises walls against the world that stands
Ready to take him up in its caressing hands.

City and night, and if there's anyone
Who watches us with love, do not forget
Him proud and helpless. When he's most alone,
And the city crowds around him desolate,
Lift up his downcast eyes; O Father, let
Your thirsty one know the redeeming taste
Of the thousand wells that stand around him in the waste.

II

Bacchus

The narrow wreath that ornaments
Laborious subtleties of hair
And straight un-Roman nose declare
A late Imperial provenance;

Purchased perhaps by a newly rich
Informer on what seemed to him
A liberal, patrician whim,
And in an ostentatious niche

Forgotten. What debaucheries
In the stifling irreligious night
Took place in its approving sight,
Under those sensual, painted eyes?

By ignorance or pious fraud
It stands now, classical, austere,
Surveying silent hallways where
Crude kouros and Cycladic god

Join in rebuke of elegance;
The bleached white of its empty gaze
Seems to the visitor to praise
A lost ancestral innocence.

The Dawn

I

Begin at the beginning—oh, I would,
If I could find one. Surely when the day
Breaks and the sun, old symbol of the Good,
Returns to its benefactions, I could say
That's a beginning—for the star I see
Is no less illuminating now than when
It summoned the Greeks to their Academy
That the dialectics might begin again;
But of course to them the sun was not a star,
And the Good with its capital was not a symbol,
And the dialogues were not read in a book;
For they had not known those colonnades of marble
As a picturesque ruin, or been taught to look
With eyes that see things simply as they are.

2

So far away! that first tranquillity,
That homeland! But it was already late
When Plato, his mind ignited, sought to free
The childish orthodoxies of the state
From ingrown and compounding error—glancing
Over his shoulder at Democritus
And misled Thales, and the false entrancing
Gods Homer foisted on the populace;
For Athens, already immemorial,
Looming between him and the primal sun,
Cast a distorting shadow on the earth,
In whose dark he struggled towards the coronal
Of the good, the true, the beautiful—the One
That could bring his ancient world a second birth.

3

But shadows are always gathering. His dark
Was a large and noble midday in the eyes
Of a homesick nineteenth century, whose work,
Hope and reward was to philosophize
With half as much Mediterranean unconstraint;
Yet those Doctor-Professors, involute, pedantic,
Were themselves a beginning, came before the taint
Settled on everything German and Romantic;
Innocent still, they plied the fundamental
Ground where the Concept, State, and History
In darkness are born, and dragged them to the light—
Brief brightness, till their grandsons brought the night
In which we still wander, and the mystery
Of nightmare descending from the transcendental.

4

Is there no beginning, then—only the rage
Of each generation at its destiny,
Dross that is forged into a golden age
By a future enraptured with what used to be?
But that would be consolation! Every dawn
Dies into dark, and from the dark is born;
And at midnight, when it seems forever gone,
The sun even then is starting to return:
So even this twilight decade, though it seems,
In the shade of the thousand years about to close,
The darkest of any known to history,
Is a kind of beginning—and our task to be
On the look-out for the first elusive gleams
Of Dawn, spreading out her fingertips of rose.

5

But of course the dawn itself is an induction,
A faith that the future will repeat the past,
That the constellations will escape destruction
Tonight at least, though we know they cannot last
Till the end of time. So let the metaphor
Of dusk and dawn be comforting, a lie
We tell ourselves in order to endure
And impose a more general order on the sky;
I will happily believe. But still recall
That once, on the hills of Argos late at night,
The beleaguered watchman saw a sudden flame
Rise in the east, and shouted his delight
To the sleeping city; but the news that came
Was only of Troy's disastrous, final fall.

Heroes Have the Whole Earth for Their Tomb

Tonight I read of an ancient war
Once thought self-evidently great,
Out-blazoning all that came before,
Each battlefield a hinge of fate,

And marvel once more at how the gain
Or loss of some extinguished city
Could cause defeated men such pain
And win for the conqueror such glory.

Who wondered then if Amphipolis
Merited agonizing death,
Or doubted that mighty Brasidas
Would, for as long as men drew breath,

Shine forth in his dear-bought renown?
And when did the majesty of act
Imperceptibly dwindle down
To indifferent, objective fact?

Athens and Sparta gripped each other
For thirty years; all those who died
Piled in a single trench together
Could not for an hour have pacified

Insatiable Passchendaele; the dead
Rise in an exponential series
From units in the Megarid
Up to the hundred thousand bodies

Now nourishing the green Ardennes.
If trophies were to be built for all,
The urns would leave no room for men,
The names would require an endless wall.

History that the Greeks released,
Unconscious of evil, from the lamp,
Now finds its scale so far increased
That atom-bomb and murder-camp

Draw less profusion from the heart
Than a few soldiers killed at sea
When Pericles, in the crowded mart,
Read out his invented eulogy.

Three Odes after Horace

I

Oh, Postumus, you crouch beneath
Your goodness as if it could be
A shield against senility,
The old-age home, blindness and death;

You brag about your discipline
Of kindness, prayer and sacrifice;
Do you think they will pay the price
The gods extort from living men?

Open your eyes! What saint or king
In all recorded history
Has been taken up bodily
To God, perched on an angel's wing?

Even if you're your body's slave—
You eat right, exercise, and sleep
With just one woman—you won't keep
Your precious self long from the grave.

No, you will leave your thriving firm,
Your wife, your car and house; not one
Of the shining projects you've begun
Will reach fruition then; the worm

Will suck your fat, while your accounts
Are drained to plump your worthy heir,
Who will be grateful you're not there
To scold as his expenses mount.

No, you will leave—and what you find
No honest man ventures to tell,
Except to guarantee it will
Be worse than what you left behind.

II

Now snow is abandoning the fields
        Before triumphant grass,
Now crumbling ice at the riverbank
        Allows the stream to pass—

As though there were a grace at play
        In the seasons' constant round,
Or voices leading springtime on
        With low and lovely sound.

But "hopeless!" is their only word
        For men who stop to hear—
The days and hours are still at work
        To carry off the year;

And the moons that die from month to month
    Are reborn in the sky,
But you are an earthly thing, and fade
    Forever when you die.

Do you remember Orpheus
    Who thought he cheated death?
And have you heard of Lycaon,
    Begging to his last breath?

All that they had, genius and wealth
    And desperate eloquence
Was dust and shadow, faced with death's
    Placid indifference.

You do not own your days—tomorrow
    Is the gods' to give,
They who delight in teaching man
    He has no right to live;

And the snows that melt will fall again
    Upon this early grass—
Remember, and take up your life
    Before it too can pass.

III

See what I've done! No skyscraper or arch
Of triumph is bolder, or will last as long;
Pollution and vandals and incompetence
Will wreck those monuments; mine will survive.
I've beaten death; as long as there are men
Who bow and scrape to genius, I will find

Priests and disciples; even in that town
Where I grew up, they'll be force-fed my odes,
And know I made it out, to conquer Rome
And train the language into finer forms.
Muse, I have earned all this. Bring on your crown;
I'm waiting, and my head is lifted high.

Washington

Another Fourth! Again the capital
Is emptied out along the Nation's Mall,
Where the elaborate fireworks display
Mounted in tribute to the holiday
Gives us the satisfaction of pure leisure
Tinged with the echo and the show of danger,
Rocket in abstract, imitated bomb,
And play of fire above the Pentagon.
We roar approval as the sky bleeds red,
Then bursts to blue and yellow; overhead
A thousand falling sparks, and in the ear
The delayed explosion, frighteningly near,
Whose force is rolled around the marble fronts
Of a hundred treasuries and monuments;
Not abstract now, but all too similar
To what we know from the reports of war
In some less favored city. All around
Nothing but thrill and happiness, the crowd
Gazing at innocent peacetime mockery
Of shell and tracer in the painted sky,
Fearing no harm, and with no cause to fear—
No bomb for two centuries has fallen here.
This city, anxious showcase capital,

Vaunting in marble its imperial
Ambitions in the midst of poverty,
Injustice, slum, crime, vice and bigotry,
Still remains standing, troubled but secure,
And seems eternal. But how many more
Decades or centuries can it expect
Of unchallenged dominion? Greater powers were wrecked,
At more auspicious moments; Rome supreme
Woke one day from her thousand-year-old dream
To find she had been ravished as she slept;
Athens' hard-mastered mastery was kept
For a lifetime only; now the opera house
Where Wagner in Dresden battled long to rouse
His Philistine nation is an office tower,
And London is warmed at the ashes of its power;
All, all are fallen. Who could think tonight,
Surrounded by shouts and whispers of delight,
Of a like fate here, of fires and sharper cries,
Echoes of ordnance, crumbling majesties
Of these palaces and monuments in flames,
Destruction of men and landmarks with their names;
Familiar roster of the antique Fall
Prepared in turn for every capital,
Or else the more modern, unexampled death
Of a hundred thousand in a single breath,
Leaving no tellers and no human tale—
Thoughts so immense the thinking has to fail.
Better to turn away, or else to try
Imagining the mundane eternity
We may build yet on earth: this city still
Decaying through time and waste of civic will,
By water and air, but not by human fire;
A modest and an impossible desire.

Across the Potomac, hidden in the night,
The Pentagon too is bathed in festive light,
But takes no notice of the holiday;
Somewhere in those impenetrable gray
And concrete barricades it labors on
With solemn duties that are never done,
Tracking and plotting, taking photographs
From the stratosphere to guide the Chiefs of Staff;
And the hidden places, ours and theirs, still bristle
With upreared columns of the wary missile,
Hair-triggered, indifferent, waiting for the call.
All this unthought of, as above the Mall
The veil is rent in miniature; and soon,
When the show is done, and once again the moon
Travels alone through the untroubled sky,
Thousands will scatter peacefully away
To home and bed, and the untroubled rest
Reserved for the not egregiously unjust—
To work and live in the mild benevolence
Of the transitory cloaked in permanence.

Goodbye to Washington

City, the unhistorical,
Built once for all on a grid of sense,
Hiding in marble monuments
A soul routine and clerical,

Instruct me — Representative
And famous unknown Senator
Have worn and taken off their honor,
Emptiest that the world can give.

General, your name now lost
As a synonym for government
Industrious, secure, content,
Skilled at the estimate of cost,

Instruct me — you who scorned a place
In Empire's rich bureaucracy,
And made of yourself a destiny,
Gorgeous, with glory on your face.

Years that I spent here, what was mine
Of impersonal or ardent hope
You took, and taught me how to cope
With real life, neither rare nor fine;

Instruct me—may I leave behind
The worldly city and Washington,
To build for myself that prouder one,
Angry and reticent, of the mind.

Y2K

I believe it could end like this: a small mistake
Made by anonymous engineers, now dead,
   And multiplied silently
    Through fifty prosperous years,

Until, as in a nightmare, evidence
Seeps to the surface like a hidden stain,
   And we realize too late
    We are victim and culprit both.

Indifferent in solidity, the earth
Looks on as we build towers on its back;
   It is happy to bear us up,
    Or take us underneath;

And the sea, indifferent in its violence,
Consents to be mastered by the mariner,
   For whether he reaches port
    Or drowns, it will rage on.

They know the year only as the repetition
Of tide and season, each so regular
    In arriving and departing
    That change is constancy;

We were assigned to give the years their names,
As we named the earth and sea and all their creatures,
    And in naming them, created
    The space for history.

Then is it an accident that what we've made
Should turn against us, and though fictional
    Destroy the apprentices
    That heedless set it loose?

Soon we will see if the world we have created
Over the placid, self-subsisting earth
    Will come to grief at last;
    But even if it survives,

I believe it will end like this: a small mistake
That the next time may prove incurable;
    We have lived by history,
    And with history will die.

Lebanon

Where was the spicy cedar sown?
Hidden in vales of Lebanon.

When and by whom were the seedlings planted?
Time out of mind at the Lord's commandment.

Why? To be cut in boards and planks
For the Temple where Israel gave thanks.

And how did they harvest it? All day,
Till the sunlit hours were worked away;

Then by lantern and candlelight,
Singing a frantic song, all night,

Drunk with the cedar and the moon
Hidden in vales of Lebanon.

The Chosen People

The moon, we know, is devious:
She leads midnight conspiracies
To influence the push and pull
Of wholesome, unsuspecting seas.

It's jealousy, of course — look how
She sits there, always pale, exiled
From the blue central teeming sphere,
Despising earth, but still beguiled.

Yet why should she complain? The fate
Of each was fixed so long ago,
And without malice; some dust-clouds
Settled above, and some below —

And these, being more numerous,
Became a planet; those, the few,
Congealed into a wandering tribe.
Now what can anybody do?

Arrangements of such magnitude
Are given, not made. We who find
That all our shame and longing won't
Make us like the rest of humankind

Should not feel slighted; after all,
Each tribe has something to resent,
And we at least are like the moon,
Lonely and strange and eloquent.

III

Autobiography

Greek at ten,
Weeping with rage
At women's reckless
Wreck of law—
The adulteress
(As on the stage)
Pries open
The Furies' maw.

Later Italian,
Wringing out
Each sob's beauty
In late-night talks,
For years devout
To one whose sin
Is that she walks
Below, like me.

Then failed French,
Trying the tricks
That others work
By self-belief.
Alas, the wrench—

Conscience berserk—
Ends in grief
Instead of sex.

And now? I think
English, perhaps—
Keeping inside,
Talking low;
Though love denied
Leads to the brink
Of a collapse,
She'll never know.

One Weekend

How many times across the centuries
Has a young man, promising, dissatisfied,
Paced an uncomprehending town at night,
Breathing contempt for everything he sees:
Church-tower and unpaved road and village square,
His whole life's limits. Just to have a choice
Of job or wife would be his Paradise—
Off in New York or Moscow, anywhere
Anonymous and prodigal. I think
Of that old script, aboard the early bus
From my suburb to your metropolis,
Trying again to reinforce the link
That our distance unravels. There's a cost
To this new life, which that maddened and bold
Young man could not predict: though you would hold
Fast to some things, you blink, and they are lost.

2

We are polite, at first—there is no name
For what we are now, no way to be sure
If some question or look has gone too far.
Things would be different, in a different time—
Married by now, unable to avoid
The anchor-weight of children, we would have
The steady-sailing and frustrated life
We all are meant for. But instead the tide
Of option and ambition washes us
So far apart that we can barely see
The outline of the face that used to be
The morning's first sight, peaceable and precious;
Which now contorts into a social smile,
And asks about a relative or friend.
How did we get here? I don't understand . . .
And shall we look at photographs a while?

3

We're free to stay up late on Sunday night,
Careless and animal, while on TV
The wheezy print of a Marx Brothers movie
Enthralls us with its battered black-and-white.
They're our ideal, and teach us to reject
The easy way of saying what we mean;
Our virtuosic back-and-forth routine
Is just as loving, just as indirect.
We watch, we never were more intimate;
Too talkative and high-strung to sit still
While our two souls slip out and intermingle,
This mutual distraction is our height

Of ecstasy, both knowing that we'll laugh
At the same punchlines. How in love we are,
Just hearing: *I can see you bending over*
A hot stove—but I can't make out the stove.

4

Impossible that our misgivings should
Be stronger than our need, so long deprived
Of touch, build-up, release. And so we dive,
With still-familiar ease, into the bed—
The situation wakens some reflex
Of what to do, things go without a hitch,
Until the moment when you turn and reach
Into the nightstand for the needed box.
I wonder, how naive am I, to think
You keep them there for my exclusive use?
(Though I know I have no right to accuse
Where I would not want to face questioning.)
It can't stop me from wanting to go on—
We're practiced, too, in drawing a kind shade
When too much looking might leave us dismayed—
But for that moment, I know I'm alone.

5

Four days is not long. You walk me as far
As the subway entrance, where our banter dies
Into momentous silence; each one tries
To summarize what's happened, what we are
To one another now. Too tender for
A casual goodbye, but still afraid
To make too much of what we've done and said,

We kiss and keep silent. Oh, there should be more!
The lines for this scene are so obvious —
I promise love, and faithfulness, and you
Say you are mine; and somehow it is true,
And we part weeping. No, that's not for us . . .
Goodbye, then. I will call. And just as I
Come down the stairs, a train is pulling up;
I glimpse a man with his girl on his lap,
His face at her neck, whispering. Goodbye.

Waking

Waking, he finds his arm
Still sore from having pressed
Her unresisting form
Tightly below the breast.

(Something said in a dream
Unconscious made him fear
She would not stay the same
For long, or lie so near.)

As though he could seize the breaths
Escaping her one by one!
Instinct clings to the sheath
Of the flame already gone.

Post-Mortem

Everything else can change; we do not change.
Now autumn branches have become spring groves,
The birds return, the cineplex invites
Old crowds to new distractions; you are not
Sitting beside me, this time, in the dark,
Watching and joking, leaning and closing in;
When I turn there is someone else, more affable,
Bathed in the screenlight, radiant, not you.
So it falls out. We break and cling and break,
And the final consummation is not hate,
Nor growing up and past to indifference,
Nor even love, but this thought of you tonight—
Like twin stars circling in the distant black,
We will pull apart, apart, and will not escape.

A Love Letter

First, the preliminaries. Let me tell
Why I will try to say these things in verse,
Which I know by experience is hardly well
Suited to heartfelt explanation; worse,
In an awkward stanza, one that cannot dwell
On a subject patiently, but must reverse
Its train of thought and mine, so that I move
Only haltingly to the final station, love.

Maybe I need exactly that impediment,
Though everyone knows that speaking from the heart
Should be like a river, onrushing, with sediment
(In this case, natural clumsy words) the part
That, caught up, proves its force; then what I said I meant
Could not be doubted as a trick of art,
But, like the stream that past its channel flows,
Would prove its sincerity by turning prose.

How natural just to speak; our situation
Is a common one (though we're fortunate to get it)
And doesn't require such willful complication,
Which cannot illuminate, but may upset it;
Better to try the three-word declaration

That could summarize all mine, if I would let it;
It's not as clever, but it still might move you
If instead of this I simply wrote "I love you."

But, like a Bible text, that simple phrase
Contains enough matter for a page of glosses;
As a slide, which to the naked eye displays
A point, in the microscope is a colossus,
It appears to mean precisely what it says,
But read as we read it, the expression loses
All obvious meaning, so that when we're through
We can't be sure of "I" or "love" or "you."

The middle term, which seems the most abstract,
Is the least confusing. It is what remains,
The one irrefutable all-enduring fact,
Through a thousand ruptures, petty shocks and strains
That can only momentarily distract,
But never part us; love waxes and wanes,
But, like the hide-and-go-seek of the moon,
It is only hiding, never really gone.

The problem—or, since it need not be solved,
The mystery—is not love but the lover;
Us, the two pronouns so deeply involved
In the transitive verb. For I cannot discover
The element in me that is not dissolved
By a change of time or place; the days are over
When I thought that attaching to my name
Was a portable essence, everywhere the same.

Think of that spring, the strange inauguration
Of the reign in which we are still living now
(Though there were interregnums, an occupation
By a foreign power). We watched the river flow
Flashingly past us, and its mute elation
Gave me the courage (still I don't know how)
To say what my odd behavior had implied,
To ask what I thought could not have been denied.

Said what? Asked what? And has it been five years
Since that first embrace, unlooked-for, wild, momentous?
The river still flows, still flashes, and still hears
From new undergraduate lips the same portentous
Soft declarations; all the world appears
To them as it did to us; their own tremendous
Hour, the one that realigns their fate,
Could be now, this day their secret, holy date.

But we cannot step again in that same river;
It has flowed past us, though it has remained
In the same course, and will remain forever
(Or at least till the city's engineers have trained
Its floods into some more practical endeavor);
For the lives we had then cannot be regained.
Today is for hypothetical new lovers,
And tomorrow their rapture also will be over.

That night we were pledged (not quite explicitly)
To love and each other. But if we have moved
So far from that spot, that life, are we implicitly
Freed from the promise our old selves approved?
Couldn't we say the contract was illicitly
Signed by two strangers, who that night had loved,

Using our names, their now-heirs and assigns,
Who are slaves to their tyrannical designs?

Or say, if that seems too much exaggeration,
We are like the ship that, in the story, sailed
To a hundred ports, and at each destination
Took on new masts in place of those that failed,
Until in the course of a ten-year navigation
Each plank was changed; when finally it hailed
The original harbor, was the ship that came
To the isle it departed different or the same?

And yet we fare forward. How? Look at the way
We talk about love, the words that do not lie;
Proclaiming it to the world we do not say
"I love," as though love depended on the I
Whose resolves can be altered twenty times a day,
But rather "I am in love," and so imply
That love, like a necessary atmosphere,
Surrounds us, pure or polluted, everywhere.

Love is a faith, though not because the lover
Sees a divinity in his darling's eyes
(Love made on that principle would soon be over,
Unless, as with Beatrice, she quickly dies);
But love becomes for him the Unmoved Mover
No logical proof explains or justifies;
He rejoices that in love at last he's found
The self-evident good, the all-sustaining ground.

Dearest, though it's taken me so long
To reach the point where I openly address you,
I already fear I've written this all wrong,

Said something unwittingly that may distress you.
If you've found anything that's true or strong,
Your presence made it so; but I confess, you
Will be justified if you are only critical,
Since all my powers, poetic, analytical,

Cannot do justice to the theme. You are
The atmosphere, the river, and the ground,
The ship, the destiny, and many more
Mysterious things for which I haven't found
Appropriate or becoming metaphors:
For a word, we've learned, is an arbitrary sound
Yoked to a meaning, and will never do
To describe what's essential, necessary, true.

So no more words. Already it is late,
And soon it will be night, and time for sleeping;
A thousand miles of darkness separate
My bed from yours, but let there be no weeping;
Time parted us, but I believe that fate
Will deliver you somehow to my safekeeping,
And trust, what is impossible to prove,
That all will be well with us and with our love.

Epithalamium

The church's walls commemorate
The hundreds of less fortunate
    Young men who did not hear
    A marriage-service there;

In Italy or France, where soon
Our friends will take their honeymoon,
    A briefer, sterner path
    Conducted them to death.

This summer afternoon, it is
Proper that they be witnesses
    To this public sacrament;
    Silent, they represent

The older virtues, and approve
The form that marriage gives to love,
    Composing present pleasure
    To a statelier, stronger measure.

Marriage, perhaps, is weaker now
That law and technology allow
    Urges we once denied
    To be instantly satisfied;

Indifference makes us tolerant
Of frailties that have always meant
    Sons' ruin, daughters' shame,
    And novels' favorite theme.

Yet only the modern couple, freed
From sexual and financial need
    That anciently condemned
    To bondage without end,

Without embarrassment can choose
To give themselves, so serious,
    Serene and dignified,
    Like this groom and bride.

Now, as they set to furnishing
Their rented rooms with everything
    Department stores supply
    And guests or parents buy,

Let their own luck and our good will
Secure them what is dearer still,
    The benefits whose price
    Is daily sacrifice:

Patience with small, familiar flaws;
Respect, when love no longer awes;
    Fidelity and trust
    Through the ordeals of lust;

May these, and what the law can give,
Marry them truly while they live,
    And solace the lonely heart
    When death shall make them part.

IV

Emblems

The dollar bill on front and back
Bears the engraver's hidden seal;
All of the counterfeiter's skill
Cannot make up its subtle lack.

Hidden in air is the single course
The shot takes to the target's eye;
A hundred thousand just near by
Lead it to failure, loss or worse.

The searchlight staggering in the dark
Illuminates nothing—look, its beams
Are prosecuting still what seems
An incomprehensible, fruitless work.

Indecision

What more on a summer afternoon
   Could I require?
Light without heat, my work-week done,
   A free desire,

And the world from my balcony composed
   Like a Renaissance
Picture, the elements disposed
   With significance

Too obvious to miss: the trees
   Are Nature's beauty;
My notebook the imperious
   Summons to Duty.

Neither could Lust's abrupt demands
   Have been omitted:
A sunbathing girl on the next roof stands,
   My gaze permitted

As though she did not notice it; and last
    The stereo
Is playing Mozart's movements, fast
    Then aching-slow,

A sign for the already adequate
    Engrossing Past.
Everything's given, though I know it
    Cannot last—

What one impetuous faculty
    Would quickly choose
The others as necessarily
    Loudly refuse.

The Body turns to her, the Soul's at rest
    In sexless nature;
Ambition writes, but Conscience knows the best
    Is done, and culture.

And so the day goes by. Is life
    Thus to be wasted,
Force spent in an internal strife
    And nothing tasted?

Our fate is not to be the sum
    Of all these joys,
But to offer them a medium
    And counterpoise.

Irresponsible Foetus

No accident—only the mute
    Accumulation
Of causes you did not suspect,
    And their quick fruition.

If at the drugstore you had reached
    For a different pack,
Or decided against the passionless
    Expected fuck,

Or even—but there is no one
    Now to hear;
Only the as yet deaf-and-dumb
    Lying so near,

Who curls like a question mark
    Beneath the breast,
Putting all you have been and are
    To the awful test.

Zoloft

There was no science for the cure of souls;
Like all our early magics, it remained
Prestigious, secret, ineffectual
Through generations of compounding pain.

Its element was darkness: in the cave
Where painted spirits flickered in the fire;
In the shadow-booth confessional that gave
The antidote for each proscribed desire;

Even the analyst's study, where the dream
Told the transactions of its wild bazaar.
All twilight glamours and invented names
To flatter our illnesses with metaphor.

We are body, to the end. Now misery
Will take its place with polio and plague,
An unclean habit or deficiency
Endemic in a less enlightened age;

While madness and possession, shame and sin
Survive, like the humors or astrology,
To make us smile at errors that have been,
Or figures to adorn our poetry.

Spring Forward

Spring in its absence seems a cure
    For winter's long disease;
In the months of less, we await the more
    That April promises.

But now that it's come, and nights are warm,
    We find there's no relief
For lust with a thousand ways to harm,
    Love's complicated grief—

Spring heats, we realize too late,
    No less than winter chills
Allow the mind to germinate
    Its fertile strain of ills.

Obedient to the world, the clock
    Runs faster. Late at night
Eyes grown accustomed to the dark
    Find the sky strangely bright,

And widen; even so, the soul
    Painfully must dilate,
Till the part of itself that it thought the whole
    Breaks underneath its weight.

Tonight it seems easier in the cold
    To scavenge sustenance
Than to venture out, erect and bold,
    To master the passing chance;

But there is no going back. The power
    Dormant in us so long
Luxuriates in this extra hour,
    And feels itself grow strong.

42 Up

The girl who knew at twenty-one
She was too strong and pure for marriage
Is pregnant, and hoping for a son
To join the girl in the baby-carriage;

The seven-year-old who in the drab
East End dreamed of the jockey's speed
Is happy to drive a taxicab
Now that he has six mouths to feed;

And of course the boy at the public school,
Born to an ancient name and grand,
Remained a simpering heartless fool
And became a solicitor, as he planned.

Some find that they cannot fight free
Of the usual domestic messes,
Some put on quiet misery
Thoughtlessly every day, like glasses;

And the last, most cherished mystery,
How I have grown to what I am,
Is stripped in the documentary
To the logic of a diagram:

Urge endowed by the mindless gene
Colliding with hopeless circumstance
Is all our various lives have been,
Mathematical, immune to chance.

Yet each of them, staring from the screen
And whispering "You are one of us,"
Defies me to say that what I've seen
Makes life any less mysterious.

Don Giovanni

Once poets wrote and Caesars staked their claims
In the tangled, lucid periods of Rome;
Astride the world, they told themselves their names
Would never die, while Latin had a home.
Who could have guessed, and who would have believed,
That a gutter dialect would reign where once
Propertius pined, Catullus was deceived,
And Horace raised monuments more firm than bronze?
Now, in another world, I listen thrilled
As the Don lays siege to an Italian wife,
In words less noble, from which men could build
This stranger art, this more uncertain life —
And lose myself in fantasies of some
Barbaric masterpiece of times to come.

Going to Bed

No use—no plugging up my ears against
The body's weary, reasonable song;
Ambition, fade, and fade, half-hearted lust,
The day is done, and I have worked too long.

Oh hands, let go—nerves, slow yourselves—the night
Rolls out its constellations in the sky;
Put out once more the artificial light,
Admit that one more day has hurried by.

And wait—and as the habit of control
Dies out between two pulses of the mind,
Something in us that passes for a soul
Will spread wide wings, and leave this life behind.

Adam Kirsch was born and raised in Los Angeles. His poems have appeared in *The Paris Review*, *Partisan Review*, *Harvard Review*, *The Formalist*, and elsewhere. A former assistant literary editor of *The New Republic*, he writes regularly about poetry for *The New Republic* and other magazines and newspapers. He lives in New York City.

The New Criterion is recognized as one of the foremost contemporary venues for poetry with a regard for traditional meter and form. The magazine was thus an early leader in that poetic renaissance that has come to be called the New Formalism. Building upon its commitment to serious poetry, *The New Criterion* in 2000 established an annual prize, which carries an award of $3000. Adam Kirsch is the second winner.

DATE DUE

28 DAY

NOV 2 5 2002

MAR 3 1 2003

MAR 0 8 2008

APR 3 0 2009

WITHDRAWN

Cat. No. 23-221

BRODART